Printed Locally at Springfield Printing Corp. North Springfield VT

green
writers
press

Giving Voice to Writers & Artists Who Will Make the World a Better Place
greenwriterspress.com

ISBN: 978-1-9505848-8-8

The artwork for this book was made using watercolor on paper.
Book design by Dede Cummings and Ellen Korbonski.

Mason
Goes
Mushrooming

by
Melany Kahn

Illustrated by
Ellen Korbonski

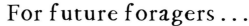

When I was growing up, my parents took me on fantastic treasure hunts for delicious wild mushrooms. They taught me which mushrooms we could safely eat, and which ones were inedible and could lead to a stomach ache, or might even be poisonous. "When in doubt, throw it out," my mom would say. "And always check with us." So I did.

My children also love to forage in the woods. Some weekends we walk with a mushroom club, and the experienced mycologists (people who study mushrooms) double-check every mushroom we find. We've even learned how to identify mushrooms through spore prints by placing mushroom caps on paper overnight. The seed-like spores that drop make a colorful design that helps identify the mushrooms.

Mushroom hunting is a wonderful way to connect to nature. You can pick mushrooms to examine, smell, touch, or make spore art. If you wish to eat any mushrooms you find, please be sure to confirm them with an experienced adult forager — and remember:

When in doubt, throw it out.

Happy hunting,

 Melany

Dedication

For my parents, Emily and Wolf,
whose love of foraging was contagious.
And to my husband and children,
who happily caught the bug.

~ Melany Kahn

To my family for their encouragement,
and for the spirits of Stark Farm,
where it all began.

~ Ellen Korbonski

SPRING

Mason peers out the window.
They're here! Tiny pink apple blossoms!
"Buddy, the trees are waking up.
I wonder if . . .

the morels are out? Let's go mushrooming!"

Mason hunts for morels under the apple trees,
searching for their golden cones with the
honeycomb texture. He scuffs aside yellow
dandelions and lifts fallen branches.
Tree after tree. Row after row.
No mushrooms.
"This is hopeless," he mutters.

There's one! Nope.
It's a shriveled apple from last fall.

Mason's stomach grumbles and
a blister is starting on his heel.
Buddy is absolutely no help.
He's too busy chasing chipmunks.

Maybe the soil is still too cold for morels?
Mason turns back, empty-handed.

Surprise! Under a toppled tree, a golden cone
pokes up from a clump of purple mint.
Mason dives down and spies dozens of morels. *Yes!*
When his basket is full he sprints right home,
eager to show his family.

"Mushrooms!" says his sister, Ally.

Mason cuts them in half to check that they are hollow inside.

"Morels," he explains, smiling.

"Someday I'll show you where to find them."

His mom fires up the pan and cooks a fluffy

mushroom omelet. Ally tastes her first morel.

She reaches for another bite.

Morel Omelet

- 1 tablespoon unsalted butter

- 6-10 fresh morels, brush-cleaned and cut in quarters

- 2 eggs, whisked in a bowl

- salt and pepper

1. Melt half the butter in a skillet over medium heat. Add morels. Sauté until tender, about 8 minutes. Season with salt and pepper and set aside.

2. Melt remaining butter in the same pan over medium-low heat. Add the eggs and cook until nearly set, then sprinkle with the cooked morels.

3. Fold the omelet over the morels and cook until done. Season to taste.

Early
SUMMER

Mason loves the 4th of July parade in his tiny town
in Vermont. When the moon rises, he watches fireworks
burst in the sky. They remind him of the thunderstorms
that will soon rumble by and soak the forest, watering
the thirsty mushrooms. Then, Mason will begin
to hunt for chanterelles.

One morning after a downpour, Buddy paws at the door.
Mason gets the hint.
"Race ya!" he shouts, taking off.
Buddy bolts out into the boggy woods and disappears.
"Buddy, come back!" Buddy is gone.
"Where are you?" Mason calls,
bounding into the ferns after him.

Through the wind in his ears
he hears a distant bark.

Buddy has chased a very fast squirrel into
a perfect circle of bright yellow mushrooms.
Chanterelles! Mason knew they could grow
in the shape of a fairy ring, but he has
never seen the pattern so clearly.

Oops! Mason forgot his basket.
Good thing he wore a bucket hat.
As he picks, Mason inspects the underside
of each chanterelle for deep ridges that run down
into smooth stems. He loves their sweet smell,
like apricot jam.

At home, noodles are on the menu, garlicky
and loaded with nutty-tasting chanterelles.
Buddy gets an extra biscuit for finding the patch.

Pasta with Chanterelles

- 12 oz spaghetti for 3-4 servings
- 20 chanterelles (more if you have them)
- 2 tbsp olive oil
- ½ cup heavy cream
- 2 cloves of garlic, minced
- ¼ cup of parsley, chopped
- salt and pepper to taste
- ¾ cup of grated parmesan cheese

1. Clean the mushrooms and slice them in half.
2. Bring a large pot of pasta water to boil.
3. Cook pasta until al dente. (Don't over cook.)
4. While pasta is cooking, add olive oil to a large saucepan and sauté the mushrooms on medium-high heat for about 7 minutes. Don't stir too much, so the mushrooms can brown. When browned, add the garlic, salt, and pepper and stir for one minute. Slowly pour in cream and stir, simmering on low heat for 3 minutes.
5. Drain the pasta and save 1 cup of water for the sauce.
6. Put pasta in a large bowl and add the mushroom cream sauce, chopped parsley, and ½ cup of parmesan. Stir to coat.
7. Add ¼ cup of pasta water, more if you like it saucier.
8. Finish with the last sprinkle of cheese and ground pepper on top.

Late
SUMMER

In August, when the days are long and the sun is hot, Mason forages for lobster mushrooms. They're named for their bold red color, but are hard to find since they grow under leaves in the forest—just like lobsters tuck under rocks on the ocean floor.

The afternoon sky is cloudy and dark, but Mason
is eager to check on his secret mushroom spot.
He named it Lobsterville, because it looks like a
town of bright red houses under the hemlock trees.
"Buddy, get the umbrella."

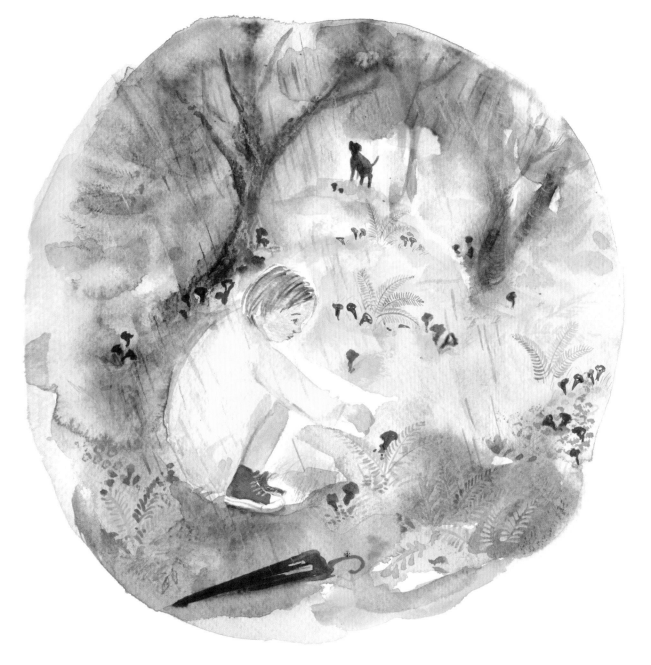

Mason spies the freckled patch just as the first
fat raindrop plonks on his cheek. He gets to work
checking each mushroom carefully, because
crawling creatures find them tasty too.

Hello, little slug!

Kaboom! A mighty clap of thunder explodes overhead.
Buddy is terrified of storms.
He whimpers, shivering beside Mason.
"I've got enough," Mason shouts. "Be brave, we'll run."

At home, the lobsters look like they've been
hauled from the ocean draped in seaweed.
"It's just dirt," Mason's mom says.
It's a lot of dirt.
Wash, rinse, slice. Repeat.
His dad sprinkles on sea salt and fries them in butter.
Mason can taste a hint of the ocean in each bite.

Lobster Saute

- 2 tablespoons unsalted butter
- 5 lobster mushrooms, well-cleaned and cut in slices
- 1 clove of garlic, minced
- salt and pepper

1. Melt the butter in a skillet over medium heat.

2. Add the lobster mushrooms and sauté until they are tender, about 8 minutes. A tip: Let them rest on each side until they brown nicely.

3. When browned, add the garlic and stir for one minute.

4. Season with salt and pepper. Serve as a side or appetizer.

AUTUMN

Many mushrooms sprout just as the leaves turn red, orange, and yellow and the apple blossoms turn into fruit.

The black trumpet mushroom is the trickiest of all
to find. It blends in with fallen leaves and becomes
invisible. But Mason learned to follow deer tracks
to black trumpets, since deer like to snack on them too.
"Let's go tracking!" Mason calls one autumn morning.
He grabs his trusty basket. Buddy leaps in circles.

Buddy sets off
with his head down and nose twitching.
They follow hoof prints to a clearing
and spy a herd of deer, who prance
off in a flash, white tails leaping.
Mason combs their grazing area.
"*Aha!*" There's
the first black
trumpet under a
curled beech leaf.
Mason gathers
a heap, but leaves
plenty for the deer.

On the way home, they rest under a great
oak tree. Mason tilts a trumpet to his ear
like it's a seashell and listens for the ocean.
Sure enough, he thinks he hears a faint
echo of waves. He lifts it to his nose
to smell the earthy scent.
Mason nudges Buddy out of his catnap.
"Let's head home, sleepyhead."

Mason and his dad get busy
cleaning the pile of mushrooms.
"Dad, the deer were so close.
I could see their whiskers!"
His dad gently tears open
the delicate trumpets.
"These are real beauties,"
he admires.

Mason sprinkles black trumpets across
baking pans. In the oven
they get crispy like fallen leaves.
He and his dad graze on the
warm chips, imagining how
they would feel on the
whiskers of a deer.

Crispy Black Trumpet Chips

- 2 dozen black trumpet mushrooms

- olive oil

- salt and pepper

1. Preheat the oven to 425°F.
2. Spread black trumpets on a
   baking pan with enough space
   to crisp.

If you have more than fits,
make another pan. Drizzle them
with olive oil and season
with salt and pepper.

3. Roast for 5-6 mins, until crisping.
   Turn them over and roast another
   4-5 mins. The chips will become
   brown and crispy. Remove from the
   oven and allow to cool, they won't
   last long!

Fun fact, the flavor in mushrooms is called umami.
Wild mushrooms should always be cooked and not eaten raw.
All types of mushrooms are exchangeable in these recipes and are just as delicious.

Mason can hear winter stirring
in the windy orchard
as he snuggles into bed.
Buddy yawns on the rug below.
Mason drifts into dreams of
apple blossoms, of fairy rings,
of baskets overflowing. Deep
in the earth, the mushrooms
rest too, waiting for spring.

Morel Mushroom

The morel cap has deep ridges that look like the honeycombs made by bees. If the cap looks correct, then slice the whole mushroom in half. A true morel will be a single hollow cavern from the tip of the cap to the bottom of the stem. Now check the trees around the morel. In the Northeast, morels mostly appear near apple trees, dying elm trees, and ash trees. The spore print is cream to light yellow in color.

There are inedible mushrooms that look like morels. The most common is a Gyromitra, or false morel. However, the false morel has a cap that is wavy and looks like a bulging blob, not a cone. The stem of a false morel also has multiple separate chambers, is *not* hollow, and is filled with a spongy substance. If you think you have found morels (or any mushroom) for the first time, have an experienced forager confirm what you have found. A false morel can make you quite sick. All morels (and all wild mushrooms) should be well-cooked before being eaten.

Chanterelle Mushroom

The chanterelle is light yellow to orange-yellow, with a solid, meaty feel. The top is round or funnel shaped. The chanterelle's most distinguishing feature is the vein-like ridges that run down vertically from the underside of the cap and look like they're melted into the stem. The smooth stem is the same color as the cap, and has no ring around it, and no bulb at the bottom. The chanterelle smells fruity, like a dried apricot. The spore print color is white to light yellow.

One mushroom that looks like a chanterelle is called a jack-o'-lantern. These mushrooms can make you ill if you eat them. The difference is that jack-o'-lanterns often sprout from tree stumps and grow in a single cluster, usually forming a connected clump. Chanterelles grow individually, and always on the ground.

Chanterelles have ridges, instead of actual gills, that start under the cap and wrinkle down the stem. Jack-o'-lanterns have deep, true gills that have a papery feel and separate the cap from its stalk.

Lobster Mushroom

Lobster mushrooms are a bold hunter's orange/red that looks out of place in nature. They are bright white inside, with a hard shell on the outside. The cap is funnel-shaped and emits a sticky goo, so it is usually covered in leaves or dirt. There are no deep gills, just lines on a bumpy surface, and the underside and stem are the same reddish color as the top. In the Northeast, lobster mushrooms are found most often around hemlock and oak trees. The spore color is white. Because of their unique color, there are no mushrooms that look like a lobster mushroom.

Black Trumpet Mushroom

Black trumpets are shaped like a funnel and are brown, gray, or black. The top edges of the mushroom are rolled outwards and are wavy, like a tulip or trumpet. They have no gills or pores or teeth, so the underside is smooth to slightly wrinkled, becoming smooth half the way down the stalk. The flesh is thin and easily broken, and feels suede-like and soft. The inside of the stem is always completely hollow. Look around for them to grow under beech, oak, and black birch trees in the Northeast. The spore print is white to pink/salmon in color.

Black trumpets have a unique appearance and no poisonous look-alikes, so they are a good mushroom for beginner foragers—but they do blend in with the fallen leaves, making them hard to find.